S0-BMB-175

HOT TIPS FOR

Cool Nails

By the SpiceBox Fun Team

First published in 2007 by
SpiceBox™
12171 Horseshoe Way
Richmond, BC V7A 4V4
Canada
www.spicebox.ca

Text and artwork copyright ©2007
SpiceBox™

All rights reserved.
No part of this publication may be reproduced, stored
in a retrieval system, or transmitted in any form or
by any means, electronic, mechanical, photocopying,
recording or otherwise, without the prior written
permission of the publishers and
copyright holders.

ISBN 10: 1-926567-23-4
ISBN 13: 978-1-926567-23-5

Art Director: Christine Covert
Designer: Morgen Matheson
Production: Garett Chan
Editorial Direction: Trisha Pope

Photography credits: Shutterstock pages: 3, 4, 6 - 22, 24-34, 39-40, 42,
45, 46; iStockphoto pages: 35, 37, 42, 46; and Stock.xchange: 35.

Table of Contents

Nails!

Push, pull, grab, stomp, step, kick, hold, scratch – your hands and feet perform thousands of tasks for you every day. Why not show them some extra appreciation for all the hard work they do by pampering them and making sure they always look and feel their best? This fabulous book and kit will teach you how to care for your hands and nails and treat your tootsies to a little TLC, as well as give you ideas for ways to glam up your look with some cool and funky nail art designs. It's time to put your best foot (and hand) forward!

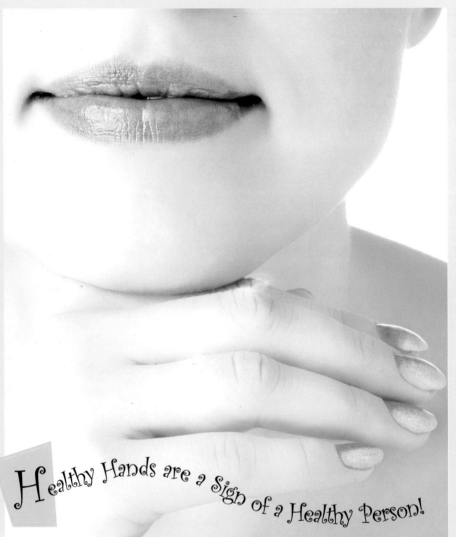

Healthy Hands are a Sign of a Healthy Person!

The care you give your hands and feet says a lot about the care you give your body. Here are some hints and tips on maintaining healthy hands and feet.

Washing:

Did you know that your hands have millions of microbes on them? And according to a survey done by the American Society for Microbiology, almost 30 percent of the adults in the USA don't wash their hands properly every day! There are lots of nasty germs that can be transferred by our hands; for example, shaking hands with someone who has a cold can spread cold and flu viruses. It is important to keep your hands clean and germ-free by washing properly as often as you can. At bathroom breaks, before and

after meal times, while hanging out at the mall, after playing with your pet, after riding a bus, escalator, or subway — find a sink and give your hands a good scrub! And don't just rinse them under the tap for a second, get them nice and wet, use some soap and work up a good lather. Another great tip is to carry a pack of wet antibacterial wipes with you, and a mini bottle of antibacterial hand gel.

❝Once you get used to keeping your hands nice and clean, you won't want to be without these handy helpers.❞

Moisturizing:
You probably already know that washing your face with soap and water strips your natural oils from your skin, which is why it is important to moisturize. The same is true for your hands. The skin on your hands is thin and delicate, and dries out easily. In fact, your hands are one of the first areas that show signs of aging. After all, your hands are one of the hardest working parts of your body!

So start now and pamper your hands with your favorite moisturizer at least once a day. Don't forget to give your hands extra protection by wearing gloves when you are cleaning, are out in cold weather, or gardening.

Keeping your feet moisturized is important as well. There is nothing less attractive when you are wearing summer sandals than heels that are cracked and scaly. A great way to moisturize is to slather on the lotion just before bed, and then put on a pair of socks. Your feet will soak up the moisture all night while you are asleep, and in the morning your toes will be soft and tender.

Sunscreen:

Don't forget to put sunscreen on your hands and feet as well as your face when you are out in the sun. Your hands will be particularly grateful for this extra care as you get older.

Normally all signs of skin damage that you can see by the time you are 30 are caused by the sun. Plan now to look young as you get older by taking precaution with your hands and face and wear plenty of sunscreen.

Nail Care: How you take care of your nails is a good reflection on how you take care of yourself! Nails quickly show the effects of poor diet by becoming thin and weak, discoloring, or becoming brittle and breaking. Make sure you eat a healthy diet, and take your vitamins! Your nails will be strong and healthy.

Nail Biting:

Nail biting is a habit which is worthwhile breaking. If you do bite your nails, please reread the section about germs; ick! If this isn't incentive enough to motivate you to stop the nail biting, try painting your nails with a lotion intended to help break this habit. Another old-fashioned method is to put dots of hot pepper sauce (such as Tabasco brand) on your nails. The pay-off for breaking this habit is lovely nails and cuticles that you can be proud to show off, as well as far fewer germs in your mouth.

Other tips to help stop the nail biting:

 Challenge a friend with the same habit to stop as well. Reward each other with manicures when you stop for good.

 Chew gum or have hard candies on hand to suck on when you have the urge to nibble your nails.

 If you bite your nails when you are at home, try putting on some lotion and a soft pair of gloves. Not only will you not bite your nails, you will have fabulously soft hands.

 Keep a nail file with you. If you bite mostly when your nail is snagged or torn, then file the problem away before you chew.

 Once you manage to grow your nails out a bit, give them a manicure right away. With a nicely filed edge and a pretty polish on, you won't want to ruin them.

Healthy Fingernails!

Fingernails are not alive, which is why it doesn't hurt to file them. They are made of layers of a protein called keratin, which is also what your hair is made of. Your nails grow from the area under your cuticle, and as new cells grow, older cells become hard and compacted and are eventually pushed out toward your fingertips. It is hard to be patient while your nails are growing out, because on average, they only grow about a tenth of an inch (3 mm) a month. It takes anywhere from four to six months for a nail to grow from cuticle to tip. That is a pretty slow process!

It is interesting to know though, that nail growth rate depends on many things.

Did you know that men's nails grow faster than women's, and young people's faster than older people's? Nails also grow faster in the summer than the winter. So if you are a young boy you may have to cut your nails every week in the summer! Your nails also will grow faster on your dominant hand (your right hand if you are right-handed) and your fingernails grow faster than your toenails. How confusing!

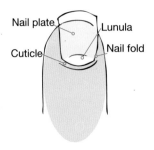

Nail plate

Lunula

Cuticle

Nail fold

This shows components
of a healthy fingernail.

Nail plate: This is the main part of the nail that we put polish on.

Nail folds: This is the skin that is all the way around the nail plate on the sides. This is often where hangnails occur.

Nail bed: Your nail bed is the skin beneath the nail plate. Cells at the base of your nail bed produce the fingernail or toenail plate. If you are clipping your nails and it is painful, often it is because you are clipping in too closely to the nail bed. This skin is sensitive so it needs to be protected by the nail plate.

Cuticle: Your cuticle is the tissue that overlaps your nail plate at the base of your nail. It protects the new keratin cells that slowly emerge from the nail bed. When this gets dry and snags it is also quite painful. So always keep your cuticles soft and moisturized.

Lunula: The lunula is the whitish, half-moon shape at the base of your nail underneath the plate.

little
Diva

What Do Your Nails and Hands Say About You?

What is the general shape of your fingertips:

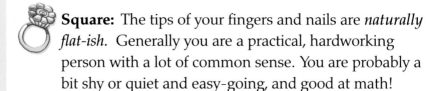

Square: The tips of your fingers and nails are *naturally flat-ish.* Generally you are a practical, hardworking person with a lot of common sense. You are probably a bit shy or quiet and easy-going, and good at math!

Pointed: The tips of your fingers and nails naturally *taper at the top*. You are the dreamer in the crowd. You are a gentle and kind person, someone who is idealistic and who is ruled by dreams, omens and superstition. You are very intuitive.

 Conic: The tips of your fingers and nails naturally are *rounded at the top*. Are you a member of your debate team or student council? If not, you should be! You are a quick thinker, a good speaker and show wisdom in your decisions.

 Spatulate: Your finger tips *narrow at the top knuckle and then are rounded at the very tip.* You are normally an active, creative and original person! You like to socialize and are a great worker.

How Flexible is Your Thumb?

Stick your thumb up and bend it backwards as far as possible, without any help from your other hand. Is it stiff or flexible?

 **Stiff thumb:** You are someone who is careful and determined, are even-tempered and have realistic expectations. Sometimes it is hard for you to trust other people.

 **Flexible thumb:** The more flexible your thumb is, the more brilliant and adaptable you are. You are happy and easy to get along with, and you are able to "go with the flow".

Which Two Fingers Have the Most Space Between Them?

Relax your hand and lay it naturally on a flat surface. Is there a larger gap between two fingers than others?

Index and Middle Finger: You are an independent thinker, form your own opinions based on the facts that you are presented, and aren't easily influenced by other people's opinions. You can be stubborn!

Middle Finger and Ring Finger: You are a free thinker, who doesn't play by any rules! You are not traditional, and have a bit of gypsy in spirit, who wants to go where the wind blows. Watch out that you don't make careless choices!

Ring Finger and Pinky Finger: You value independence and like to go it on your own. You are a bit of a mystery to your friends and family, because you don't discuss your thoughts easily, and seldom ask for help. Your confidence in yourself is a great thing, but be careful not to be inconsiderate!

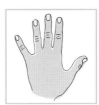

Manicures!

A basic manicure requires the following:
Bowl of warm soapy water
Hand towel
Nail polish remover
Cotton balls
Fingernail clippers
Emery board
Moisturizer
Washcloths
Nail brush
Nail buffer or
Nail polish

Set your equipment on a flat surface — by a sink is a handy place to give yourself a manicure. Cover the surface with paper towel, just in case there are any spills or drips. Anyone who has accidentally knocked over a nail polish bottle knows it isn't a lot of fun to clean up!

1. Remove any old nail polish using nail polish remover (try to find acetone-free polish — it won't dry your nails out) and a cotton ball. After it is all off, give your hands and nails a good wash with warm water and soap.

2. Trim your nails with a nail clipper if they are too long. Note: Fingernail clippers will trim in a curved line. Toenail clippers trim straight across. If you have a hard time with this step (particularly when you are trimming the hand you write with) ask a parent or friend to help. You don't want to trim below the white part of your nail as it is very painful and can lead to an infection!

3. Use your emery board to shape your nails. Go slowly and gently with this step, filing in one direction only. If you file back and forth, you weaken your nails and can damage them. You can either file straight across with only slightly smoothed edges for a "French manicure" look, or round and smooth the sides for a tapered, elegant look

4. Fill your bowl with warm soapy water. For an extra treat, add a few drops of your favorite scented oil, if you have one. Soak your hands for 5 minutes to clean your hands and moisturize your nails. If you have stubborn grime under your nails, use a nail brush part way through your soak to gently rub under your nails and clean them. Soak some more!

5. Rinse the soap off your hands. Take two washcloths and wet them with warm water. Squeeze some moisturizer on your hands, and gently rub it in, not forgetting your nails and cuticles. Tuck the warm damp washcloths around your hands and let them sit and soak up the lotion for a minute or two.

6. Fold up one of the washcloths and use a corner of it to gently push back your cuticles. Salons will often use little pointy sticks with cotton on the end of them to do this step, but a washcloth is much gentler, won't do any damage and doesn't hurt!

7. Buff or polish your nails for a shiny, healthy finish.

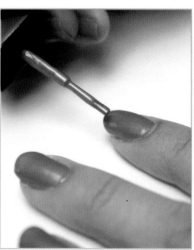

Buffing Your Nails

A nail buffer looks a lot like an emery board, but is smooth. Rub the softest side of your buffer against the surface of your nail in little circles. Once you are done this, give your nails a quick rinse to remove any "nail dust" and then smooth a drop of moisturizer or baby oil into your nails. Your nails will look healthy and shiny!

Polishing Your Nails

There are some tricks to make polishing your nails easier.

 Choose quick drying nail polish. It really does dry more quickly!

 Before opening, roll the bottle a few times, rather than shaking it. Rolling will mix it without creating little bubbles that shaking will create.

 Before painting, wipe the excess polish off the brush, or globs of polish will seep into the sides of your nails. It is easier to add a coat than to clean up a mess!

 Start by painting one stripe down the center of your nail. Then add the next strokes to each side of the middle one.

 The most important tip is to let your polish dry completely before adding another coat or doing the other hand. Have your favorite magazine handy to keep you busy and from being tempted to paint too soon!

Don't blow on your nails to help them dry — it will dull the shine of your polish.

 Don't press down too hard when applying a second or third coat or the brush will lift off the base coat.

 Once all of your coats are on and dry, use a cotton swab dipped in polish remover to clean up the edges of your fingers. Don't pick at the polish or you will end up giving yourself a hangnail!

 Always be sure to put the lid on tightly between coats. Knocking over a bottle of polish is easy to do, but hard to clean up!

Pedicures

Basic Pedicure:

Get your feet in tip top shape for summer sandals with a pedicure. You will need the following:

Bowl of warm, soapy water, large enough for your feet
Hand towel
Epsom salts or essential oils

Nail polish remover and cotton balls
Toenail clippers
Pumice stone or callus remover
Moisturizer
Washcloths
Nail brush
Nail polish

1. Use a cotton ball and nail polish remover to remove any old nail polish from your toe nails. If your cuticles are really dry, rub a cuticle cream or olive oil into them to soften them.

2. Use toenail clippers (not fingernail clippers) to trim your toenails straight across. Gently file the corners so they are slightly rounded.

3. Position a bowl of hot soapy water in front of a comfy chair. Pour in a half cup of Epsom salts, or a few drops of essential oils.

4. Fold your hand towel and place it in the bottom of the bowl. This gives your feet a nice, comfortable base to rest on. Soak your feet for five minutes.

5. Dry your feet off gently and use a pumice stone or foot file to rub off the dry skin on the bottom of your feet around your heel and base of your toes. Rinse your feet again and dry off.

6. Using the corner of a washcloth, as you did in your manicure, gently push back the cuticles around your nails and rub the area with a small amount of exfoliating scrub to clean it.

7. If you wish to have your cuticles trimmed around your toenails, it is best to have it done at a salon. It is easy to damage them and the result could be ingrown toenails.

8. Finally, rub a rich moisturizer into your feet and let it soak in. Use soap and water to wash the moisturizer off of your toenails, and you are now ready to polish them. To paint your toenails, follow the instructions for painting your fingernails on page 29.

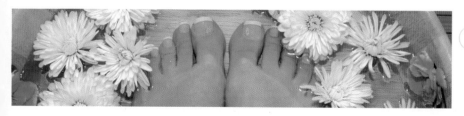

Manicure and Pedicure Party

Be nice to your hands and nails and treat them to a manicure at least once a month. This is a great time to invite a few friends over for an afternoon of pampering; it is a lot of fun to set up your beauty shop and give each other treatments.

Here is what you will need:

 All the supplies you need for a basic manicure and pedicure.

Comfy seats for yourself and your "client", as well as a table, and good lighting; either a desk lamp or overhead lights for your nail treatments.

 More comfy seats and either a footstool, a box with a pillow perched on top, or something that you can prop feet on for a pedicure treatment. Even better is a lounge chair from your patio, draped with a few fluffy towels on it to create a true "spa" feel to the room!

 The latest magazines for you and your friends to read while you are soaking or waiting for polish to dry.

 Yummy treats which are easy to eat without getting your hands messy. Chocolates, candies and drinks to sip are a great idea!

Nail Art

Once your hands look healthy, and your nails neat and tidy, you may want to add an extra bit of flair to your nail care by creating unique and stylish nail art. There are many ways to dress up your nails; use these ideas and your imagination to create a look that is all yours!   Let's look at some simple nail art designs that are easy to create and look great.

Start out with stripes. These designs are simple to create using stripes of your favorite colors. With the shades of pink and glittery polish, these nail designs remind us of yummy jelly candies. How sweet!

Two tones and dots are a great way to wear your favorite team colors! For this design paint your nails with two colors on a diagonal. Then dot two different colors along the join. Be sure to let the base color dry properly before adding the dots. With this design the base color is solid and the dots run down the center in shades of blue and white. To make dots, use a fine paintbrush or the tip of a toothpick.

Paisley shapes are fun to make, and are the perfect finish to your boho-chic look. Try darker base colors like this bronze shade, eggplant or navy.

Glittery polish is pretty and sophisticated. Try matching it with a pearl color in a similar shade for a sweet finish. The wavy stripe between the colors was made with a small paintbrush to make it easier to control.

Triangle tips. This is a fun and easy look to achieve. Paint on your base color, leaving a triangle tip. Fill that in with a contrasting color and then outline in white. Experiment with different color combinations to compliment your wardrobe.

Happy Holidays!

Celebrate each festive occasion with fabulous nails. These designs are a bit more complicated but are sure to help you celebrate with style.

Why not try a Christmas tree at Christmas? The ornaments are made by carefully gluing on individual nail gemstones and really will help you get into the holiday spirit.

This adorable Easter egg design is sure to put a smile on the Easter bunny's face! Paint your entire nail white and then decorate like an Easter egg with pretty spring colors and little nail stickers in fun shapes and styles.

Boo! How about a scary ghost for Halloween parties? By painting your nails black and then adding your ghost in white, your nails are sure to be a hit at any haunted parties.

Nothing says love on Valentine's Day like a heart and cupid's arrow. Use a skinny paintbrush or toothpick to create the detail of the arrow. Don't wear your heart on your sleeve this year; wear it on your nails!

Don't get caught without the green this St. Patrick's Day. Paint your nails with green glitter and shamrocks and you will certainly have the luck of the Irish.

Names on Your Nails!

Try painting your name on your nails. These pretty nails each have a letter of a name on them, decorated with nail stickers.

Another fun idea is to have a manicure party with your closest friends and paint your names on each other's nails. Everyone will know who your circle of best and most loyal pals are!

Gemstones Rock!

Gemstones are super popular as nail decorations and are easy to use. You can use stickers that have gemstones on them. All you need to do is peel and stick. Or you can add individual nail gemstones to your designs. You can purchase loose nail gems at drugstores in sets that come with correct glue that you need to apply them to your nails. Follow the directions carefully when you are applying them.

Combine gemstones with glitter, other nail stickers and painted patterns to get a huge variety of sophisticated looks that are simple to create.

Glitter Galore

Use glitter polishes to give your nails a little extra "bling" and sparkle. The simplest way is to use a solid base coat, and then to paint a layer of clear glitter polish over top. Or you could dab glitter on just the tips of your nails or in specific spots. No matter how you use it, be prepared to shine!

Marbling Your Nails

Marbling is easy to do and creates a really unique look. Choose two colors of polish and paint half of your fingernail with each color. Work quickly so the polish doesn't dry. Once the two colors are on your nail, use a toothpick to swirl the colors into each other. Try not to over mix the two colors or the color will turn muddy.

Flourishing Fingernails!

Celebrate summer with a host of flowers! Flowers are pretty, colorful and feminine. You can create a huge variety of looks with pretty petals, like the ones on these pages.

Cheerful Daisy: Paint your base color and then brush on thin petals of white, radiating out from a yellow center. This looks great on any background color; try green or blue for a totally different look!

Petal Tips: We painted a pink base and then added a blue glittery color on the nail tip. Where the two colors join, use a toothpick to dot on white flower petals and a yellow daisy center. How cute!

French Manicure

A French manicure is the perfect way to finish your nails when you want a look that is elegant and classy, and will perfectly suit any look you create. It is easy to do, particularly if you use the manicure guides that are in the kit.

First, choose a base color that you like and apply it. We recommend a pale pink or peach the first time you do this. You, of course, can use any color you like, but these colors are the traditional ones.

After your base coat has completely dried, carefully apply the manicure guides across the tips of your nails. The top of each guide should more or less be at the top of your nail plate. Be sure to press the guide down along both sides of the nail, as well as the top.

With an opaque white polish, carefully paint the tips of each nail, above the nail guide. You may need to apply more than one coat. Let these coats dry thoroughly before you remove the guides. Once the guides are removed, paint the entire nail with a clear coat of polish to seal.

You can of course, further embellish your nails with stickers, gemstones or other decorations. You can also try other color base coats and tip colors!

Ooh-la la! C'est trés magnifique!

You now have lots of hints, tips and ideas to help you create fabulous looking nails. We hope you enjoy creating, painting, and sharing your designs.

Have fun!